GREEK SCULPTURE
from the 16th to the 2nd Century B.C.

FONTANA UNESCO ART BOOKS

Edited by Peter Bellew

Greek Sculpture
FROM THE 16TH
TO THE 2ND CENTURY B.C.

François Chamoux

COLLINS in association with UNESCO

The art of the Greeks is a major factor in any account of the history and development of the cultures of mankind as a whole. It has had a very deep influence on the formation of a specifically European taste and sensibility and only in very recent times have art forms emerged in those countries that shared its legacy which diverge in any fundamental sense from the canons it established. It is for this reason that Greek art seems so close and so accessible to us today, although this impression of proximity to ourselves is, in part at least, erroneous for the simple reason that Greek art like all other forms of art was closely bound up with the society from which it sprang and it is only through a thorough understanding of that society that its art can really be understood.

As a result, this brief survey places a good deal of stress on the historical relevance of the works of art selected to illustrate it. To see art in terms of some basic premise divorced from time and place, as the product of some abstract human conception, is both unjust and irrational. Only by situating the art of a vanished culture firmly in its historical and natural context can we fully understand and appreciate it.

Greek art was the product of an exceptionally brilliant and lasting civilisation. It can be traced throughout a period of two thousand years from its beginnings in the first Mycenean works of art dating from the sixteenth century B.C. right up to the start of the sixth century A.D., when the rise of the Byzantine Empire gave birth to a new culture combining the legacy of Greece with Roman tradition and with Christianity.

Throughout the course of this long history the development of Greek art can be traced continuously and without a break and this in spite of violent political upheavals. Neither the Dorian invasions which destroyed the splendours of the Mycenean kingdoms, nor the Roman conquest which followed on the unparalleled flowering of art in the classical period, disrupted the continuity of an art so closely bound up with a race which had preserved its essential unity intact for centuries in the face of outside influences and foreign domination. During its final phase, when it was absorbed by Roman imperialism, Greek art lost none of its essential characteristics; its fundamental vitality revealed a capacity for renewal which enabled it in turn to give rise to the art of Byzantium.

Historians have only recently become really aware of this extraordinary continuity. For a long time the fame of the classical period—the age of Phidias and Pericles—and later the compelling beauty of the archaic period, exemplified by the *korai* of the Acropolis (Plates 10 to 13) tended to obscure the immense range of Greek art during its two thousand years of development. But nowadays nobody can ignore it however much they may prefer to concentrate on the most brilliant periods.

These generalities are an essential preliminary if the outline that follows is to be seen in its proper perspective. Moreover, Greek art will be discussed solely in terms of one particular medium, sculpture, and only some of the major stages of development will be described in relation to those works illustrated here.

It may well be asked why sculpture has been chosen in preference to other art forms? The immediate answer is purely practical in that sculpture and pottery are, with very few exceptions, the only works of art which have survived. The great works of architecture now exist only as ruins which are extremely difficult to interpret in terms of their original structure; the masterpieces of Greek painting—and painting was just as highly prized as sculpture—have disappeared completely, whereas numerous sculptures, many of them damaged and incomplete it is true, survive today and are representative of the art as a whole as well as being in many cases of the very highest quality.

But quite apart from this consideration, sculpture played an important and essential rôle in Greek society. It provided the principal expression of a religious vision which saw the gods in human form. Just as the temple—the dwelling place of the gods—was the highest task of the architect, so a religious statue embodying the Greek vision of the divine was that of the artist. The image is central to anthropomorphic religion because to a greater or lesser degree it becomes identified with the god it portrays, and it is directly to the cult-image that the worshipper addresses his prayers and offerings. Within a Greek sanctuary it was the statue which provided the focus of attention and worship, which was prized and venerated. It is therefore understandable that Greek art was preoccupied with this overwhelming need to give the divine a recognisable human form. In addition to the cult-image, which was the response to strictly-defined religious requirements circumscribed by tradition, the sculptor was called upon to provide other necessities of religious life. These included votive offerings (which frequently took the form of statues representing the god or his client), funeral monuments intended to portray throughout eternity the ideal image of the dead, and decorations for religious buildings which usually took the form of episodes from the legends of the gods in response to the highly-developed taste for narrative representation which was characteristic of the Greek mind.

We ought, however, to make no mistake about the artist's place in Greek society. Although he provided it with one of its primary means of self-expression, his function remained essentially that of an artisan and a craftsman dependent first and foremost on his manual dexterity and as such sharing the relative contempt felt by cultivated Greeks for all forms of practical pursuit with the exception of politics, war and related activities. Artists, even when their talent was held in high esteem, were never granted the status accorded to scholars, philosophers and poets. Artists were regarded as skilled craftsmen able to reproduce in a given material the religious

7

and aesthetic conceptions of the community. In no sense were they regarded as geniuses or in any way inspired. Within the choir of the nine Muses there was no Muse presiding over the plastic arts. The artist's place in society was that of a technician who, according to his rank, was able to fulfill the requirements of the group and of individual patrons without aspiring to an independent or personal rôle. It never crossed the mind of the artist to attempt to assert his own independence or his personal identity. The *artiste maudit*, the artist in revolt against society, was completely unknown in ancient Greece. The artist was simply and solely a conscientious craftsman fulfilling the same function his father or his master had fulfilled before him. Complete harmony existed between art and society.

This attitude goes a long way towards explaining the high average quality of Greek art. Convinced that their craft was far more important than inspiration, sculptors did their best work by applying workshop techniques that they had acquired in the course of a long apprenticeship, taking no account of time or difficulties, and by subordinating their own private inclinations to the demands of the prevailing taste or the collective task. Archaeologists today try without success to distinguish the different hands that had a part in creating great monumental sculptures like those on the Parthenon at Athens (Plates 18 to 20) or the mausoleum at Halicarnassus. The failure of every attempt to allocate responsibility for different parts of the total work in this way, in spite of the sophistication of technical and stylistic methods of analysis, is the most convincing proof that Greek sculptors in marble were able to modify their individual styles in accordance with the directives of a master craftsman, especially one as great as Phidias. But it must be made absolutely clear that this was in no sense a painful act of self-abnegation: it was the wholly spontaneous compliance of the individual Greek with the social laws of the community to which he belonged.

Greek sculpture is therefore totally representative of the society from which it sprang. But again it is essential to understand properly what it really has to say to us today, because it is all too easy to interpret it wrongly. Any work of art with an unmistakable meaning for the audience it was originally made for, an audience accustomed to symbolic language, faces us today with problems of interpretation that can only be solved by scholarship. Take, for example, the famous relief of *Athena* in the Acropolis Museum (Plate 17). Dating from the fifth century B.C., it is known as the *Mourning Athena* and has for many years baffled scholars who have as a result given free rein to their imagination in attempting to interpret its meaning: is the goddess contemplating some mysterious rite at the threshold of a sanctuary? Is she sadly reading a list of fallen warriors? Is she contemplating an object which has since vanished from the pillar she is leaning towards? These different views can now safely be ignored since it is known, thanks to conclusive comparisons made with contemporary vase paintings, that the relief represents none of these scenes. The pillar is the boundary stone marking the finishing line in the stadium and the goddess—quite without any trace of melancholy—is shown beside this symbol of the race because the relief is the votive offering of an athlete who had won in the games. Similarly, the celebrated bronze known as the *Ephebe of Anticythera* (Plate 25) in the National Museum at Athens has acquired a new and accurate meaning since it has been shown that it represents Hercules picking the golden apple from the miraculous tree in the Garden of the Hesperides. This particular legendary incident had a clear eschatological meaning in Greek religion; it symbolised the promise of eternal life for those who, like Hercules, were capable of surmounting the trials of earthly life. The image of the hero-god is not therefore, as was once thought, an outstandingly beautiful study of a naked athlete, but a pledge of immortality.

It would not be difficult to provide many similar examples to show that scholarship is vitally important to any complete understanding of Greek sculpture. It is all the more necessary when the work in question is damaged or mutilated and thus requires a considerable effort of the imagination to restore it to its original appearance. An equally important fact, all too often overlooked, is that all Greek sculpture was polychromatic. Every piece of sculpture that has survived (with the exception of some terracotta statues which have not lost their colouring) no longer appears to us as it did to those it was made for because all statues in stone or marble were painted in bright colours which have either disappeared entirely or survived as barely recognisable traces. The familiar image of a pure form in white marble in no way corresponds to historical reality and at no time formed any part of the Greek aesthetic ideal. On the contrary, the Greeks took supreme pleasure in the interplay of tones of pure colour which accentuated the depth of a relief, making the details stand out and therefore making them more easily decipherable. This fondness for bright colour schemes tended moreover to move in the direction of an unsophisticated realism which is one of the principal characteristics of Greek art. When one thinks for instance of a sculptor as eminent as Praxiteles, renowned for the delicacy and skill of his work, attaching such importance to the colouring of his work that he sought the collaboration of Nikias, one of the most famous painters of his time, the point becomes dramatically clear.

The same importance was attached to the colouring of bronze statues which no Greek ever saw covered with the green patina that is nowadays so admired. In fact every effort was made to prevent this oxidation of the surface which can destroy the fine detail made by the burin on the surface of the finished bronze. The original colouring of the material called to mind the brightness of gold, while the effect of realism and the vividness of the whole colour scheme were accentuated by inlays of copper or silver and—particularly for the eyes—coloured stones or glass.

Even more striking must have been those colossal masterpieces known to us only through written accounts and obviously the subject of enthusiastic admiration—the great statues in gold and ivory known as 'chryselephantine' which the religious piety of the Greeks caused them to

Funerary stele. c.500 B.C. *Height: 1 m.; upper width: 0,73 m.;*
lower width: 0,75 m. National Museum, Athens.

commission from the finest sculptors for placing in the major temples. These huge structures, sometimes thirty or forty feet in height, were supported by an internal framework of wooden beams. They combined the work of sculptors, goldsmiths, ivory carvers and jewellers. A basic wooden form was carved in detail and then covered with thin gold plaques, either chased or embossed, and thin plaques of carved ivory. The final result was a vivid contrast between the whiteness of the ivory covering the exposed parts of the body—face, arms, hands, feet—and the gold of the draperies and accessories. Other details such as the eyes were filled in with precious or semi-precious stones. The total effect when seen in the half-darkness of the inside of a temple where the only light came through the doors, must have been awe-inspiring indeed: the great statues of Buddha in some of the pagodas of the Far East enable us to experience something akin to their richness and grandeur. This almost excessive taste for colour and luxurious materials bears not the slightest relation to the pallid marbles and corroded bronzes preserved in museums today, which are merely faded reflections of the glorious sculpture of the ancient world.

It is generally accepted nowadays that Greek art origi-nated around 2000 B.C. with the Mycenean kings in Argolis whose graves have been discovered intact together with all their treasures. These royal graves date from the sixteenth century B.C. and provide the first evidence of Greek sculpture in the golden masks (Plate 1) which covered the faces of the dead warrior-chieftains buried in them. These masks were not, as has frequently been asserted in the past, moulded from the actual features of the corpse—a technique that would have been impossible with the kind of sheet metal used—but worked in repous-sé, considerable care being taken to reproduce the features of the individual concerned. The art they reveal achieves its effect by means of a determined simplification, which aims at reproducing the essentials and using where neces-sary conventional signs such as the almond-shaped raised line surrounding the eyes and the summary symbol indicating the ears. From this method is derived a singular strength of expression which enables us to sense the power and authority these warrior-chieftains possessed during their lifetime. Moreover, these Mycenean funeral masks already reveal that balance between realism and stylisation which is a typical feature of Greek art. It is found again some three centuries later in a painted stucco head (Plate 2) also from Mycenae. The modelling of the features reveals the same urge to simplify, while the tight-lipped mouth expresses the same self-assured authority and in addition the well-preserved colouring brings out the importance of colour to a form of plastic art that clearly intends to produce a particular effect. The fixed stare of the almond-shaped eyes, the elegance—albeit somewhat barbaric—of the red 'beauty spots' decorating the chin and cheeks are not easily forgotten. The strangely obsessive features of this early head contain in embryo the colossal temple statues of the classical period over a thousand years later.

Coming originally from the north, the Myceneans had been strongly influenced by Crete which had for many centuries had a flourishing culture that was as brilliant as it was original. The cultural influence of Crete spread through trade and conquest to the tribes and principalities of mainland Greece. They not only borrowed Cretan techniques but also adapted certain specifically Minoan cultural traits such as the taste for narrative art, for movement in art and even the feeling for nature revealed in unobtrusive landscape backgrounds. These typically Minoan characteristics were however modified by the Greeks' own taste for simplification intended to produce a monumental effect. The golden drinking cups, decorated in relief and found at Vaphio in Laconia (Plate 3), may have been made by a Cretan goldsmith because the scenes of bull hunting and work closely resemble genuine Cretan work, but their presence in the Peloponnesus shows the source of Greek inspiration during the Mycenean period. Thus from the very beginning of the second millennium B.C. the two principal characteristics of later Greek sculpture are already present: statues in the round anticipated in the golden death masks and modelling in relief in the Vaphio cups.

We must now pass over a period of more than six hundred years from the thirteenth century B.C. to the seventh, when Greece seemed to have lost the tradition of plastic art on a monumental scale. Only bronze or terracotta statues of modest dimensions—although often extremely expressive in their systematic stylisation—show that Greek craftsmen had retained their feeling for form and carving in relief. This was a time of rapid change because of political divisions, fresh invasions of Greek-speaking tribes from the north and the activities of pirates in the Mediterranean. The Mycenean kingdoms disappeared and were gradually succeeded by a crowd of small city states. Only when these states became prosperous in the second half of the seventh century, was there a renaissance of monumental sculpture. The same period saw the building of the first of the temples whose remains are visible today. Up to this time only pottery had provided artists with enough scope for experiment and development, or at least so it would seem from the specimens that remain. Ivory carving also continued to flourish but not enough examples have survived to enable us to evaluate it properly. In compensation for this lack of evidence, the end of the seventh century saw the reappearance of large-scale sculpture with works that are as impressive in their proportions as they are in their high aesthetic aims. Athens, where the potters of the preceding Homeric period had produced vases on a monumental scale, was the centre for this transposition into marble sculpture of this taste for grandeur. The head found in the cemetery of the Dipylon is over a quarter larger than life size and the statue to which it belonged must have been over eight feet high. Even more colossal was the statue discovered at Cape Sunium at the eastern tip of Attica which was eleven feet high. These alone are clear evidence that towards 600 B.C. Greek sculptors in marble were capable of carving these huge blocks into representations of the human form.

These early statues all portray a young male nude

(Plate 4), known in Greek as *kouros* (plural *kouroi*). They were directly inspired by the Hellenic ideal of the athlete which found its practical expression in the Olympic and other competitive games—a theme which continued to preoccupy sculptors until the end of the classical period. Their main aim was either to depict a god in idealised and perfect human shape or to represent a worshipper of a god, when the statue was intended to be a votive offering (Plates 5) or, again, when it was a funerary monument to provide a faithful portrait of the deceased. But in every case it is the idealised aspect that is most prominent: the portrayals of the human body are at some remove from immediate individual characteristics and are intended to make eternal an image of strength and beauty at their height of perfection. Gods are modelled on men and men are shown approximating to the perfection of gods. The artist is thus obliged both to make a close study of nature in order to reproduce its marvellous harmony and at the same time to transcend reality in order to convey an impression of the supernatural. This delicate balance and interplay between realism and the idealised forms required by an anthropomorphic religion was endemic to Greek art from the very start and the Greek enthusiasm for this quality never diminished.

Throughout the sixth century B.C., the golden age of archaic sculpture, the *kouros* figures show an uninterrupted development. The *Kouros* of Milo (*c.* 550 B.C.) reveals a tendency towards a greater elegance of form by a lengthening of the entire figure, and a quarter of a century later the same tendency is visible in the bronze statue of Apollo (originally carrying a bow in his left hand) recently discovered in Piraeus (Plate 6). The face of the god, benign, redolent of nobility, is a perfect representation of the idea of a god in human form that was held by the Greeks of that period. It is also a remarkable technical achievement and reveals clearly that the bronze founders had obtained complete mastery over the lost wax method of casting and were capable of producing works on a large scale. In subtle contrast to this imposing statue is a marble *kouros* found near Anavyssos in Attica (Plate 7).

This is a funerary statue and represents the deceased as an athlete, but there is little discernible difference between the divine and the human when it is compared with statues clearly intended to represent gods. Even in the representation of animals (Plate 8) the artist of this period achieved either a supreme elegance or a magisterial authority.

Alongside the statues in bronze and marble, reliefs of the period provide ample evidence of the virtuosity of archaic sculptors. Some of these depict the same subjects as sculpture; for example the funerary stelae such as that of the warrior Aristion (Plate 9) which dates from about 520 B.C. This particular piece is characterised by a rather stilted elegance verging on the calligraphic which must have been further set off by a delicate polychromatic treatment. The name of the artist is carved at the base of the stele and this attribution to an individual represents a momentous change. This affirmation of the artist's individual identity is an innovation introduced by Greek artists into a world which had hitherto attached no importance whatsoever to the personality of the artist. It revealed itself simultaneously in sculpture and in painting and remained thereafter as a dominant feature of art in the western world.

The sculptors of the archaic period were as skilled in the portrayal of feminine grace as they were in the portrayal of the elegant strength of young male athletes. The delightful group of votaries of Athena excavated on the Acropolis is justly famous. The group of maidens (usually known as *korai*), clothed in their festive garments (Plates 10 to 13), reveals a matchless variety. Their faces are lit by a smile which may seem no more than a stylistic convention but which is in fact genuinely representative of the Greek spirit. The smile indicates that the sculpture portrays a human individual filled with a real interior life, a being capable of feeling, a creature truly alive and not merely a cold likeness. The artist was not endeavouring to produce an exact physical resemblance, but to evoke the living worshippers of the goddess. All these young women, some obviously rustic, others more sophisticated, were made up with cosmetics and dressed in brightly-coloured clothes and jewellery—an ensemble designed to raise the spirits and charm the eye of the beholder.

The transitional period between the archaic and the classical is dominated by the personality of Phidias; its art is categorised by scholars as the 'severe style'. Chronologically it corresponds to the first half of the fifth century B.C. and its taste, in contrast to the serenity of archaic sculpture, tends towards a grave austerity which is particularly evident in the expressions of the faces of statues and figures sculpted in relief. Moreover, there is a marked unity of style which contrasts forcibly with the variety of the preceding schools and styles.

The discipline evident in the severe style was undoubtedly a direct consequence of the menace of Persian invasion faced by the Greeks in 490 B.C. and again in 480. The memory of this period of trial exerted a profound effect on Greek sensibility and gave rise to a new collective awareness of common dangers and common bonds among all the Greeks. The sculpture of the period reflects this collective awareness together with the new dynamism produced by the Greek victory over the Persians. The images of the gods possess more grandeur of conception and show less magnanimity, while the artists show clearly the degree to which they were seeking passionately complex and difficult effects. No single work of art reveals this more clearly than the famous bronze recovered from the harbour of Histiaea (Plate 14). It portrays Poseidon, god of the sea, who is shown brandishing his trident (although this has not survived) in readiness to strike an enemy or perhaps simply to calm the turbulence of the ocean with a menacing gesture. The sculptor has given maximum emphasis to the movement of the limbs: the legs are wide apart and extended in a forward stride, the right arm reaches back ready to strike with the trident, while the left arm is fully extended towards the object of the blow. It conveys an impression of irresistible strength that matches perfectly Aeschylus's " god who reigns over the oceans, wielder of the never-failing spear " which was written at roughly the same time, about 460 B.C. The sculptor, like the poet has given expression to the ideal of an entire culture.

As well as the great statues of the gods like the *Poseidon* of Histiaea, the severe style produced magnificent images of victorious athletes, such as the famous *Charioteer* from Delphi whose interior tension beneath an apparently calm exterior is no less impressive than the regal movement of the *Poseidon*. Great artists then flourished; Kritios, to whom a marble ephebe (Plate 16) found on the Acropolis is attributed, and, a little later in time, Myron, who is famous for his *Diskobolos (The Discus Thrower)*. Myron's aim in this particular statue was clearly to capture the instantaneous quality of the movement immediately before the actual throwing of the discus by means of an exact analysis of all its constituents. The critics of the ancient world defined the principal criteria governing this search for precision as rhythm and symmetry. While we have no precise understanding of what they meant by these terms, it is clear that these are abstract notions which attempt to rationalise the intellectual activity in the mind of the artist when he is confronted with the complexity of models taken from nature on which he seeks to impose his own aesthetic order. This art, so abundantly aware of natural forms, is nevertheless steeped at the same time in intellectual analyses of them. Take for example the small bas-relief of the *Mourning Athena* (Plate 17) mentioned earlier. The folds of her dress do not fall in vertical lines as they would if the laws of gravity were precisely observed; instead they follow the oblique movement of the body—yet the attitude of Athena leaning on her spear seems utterly natural and relaxed. By consciously and deliberately departing from objective reality the artist has transcended nature and achieved a deeper truth—a process that is typical of Greek art.

The severe style laid the foundations for the achievement of the greatest genius of Greek sculpture: Phidias. Raised among the daring experiments of the period, he completely absorbed them and exploited their lessons with consummate skill. He softened the initial severity of the dominant style while at the same time enabling it to reach its finest expression. While his contemporary, Polykleitos, was primarily concerned with producing bronzes of athletes, Phidias remained essentially a 'maker of gods'—as the critics of the ancient world wrote of him, " he enriched traditional religion ". This enrichment is above all apparent in the great statues of ivory and gold which remain his chief claim to fame. They include the Olympian *Zeus* and the *Athena Parthenos*. The delicate assemblage of different materials and the combination of different techniques which went into the creation of these statues has already been described, but Phidias combined in his own person the skills of the sculptor, painter, goldsmith and even the architect in his conception and execution of these colossal works. His contemporaries and posterity alike throughout the period during which his two major works survived never ceased to admire them unreservedly as if they represented the definitive and perfect incarnation of the divine.

Trying to imagine them today all that we have to go on are the descriptions of Pausanias, a traveller of a much later period who described them in the second century A.D., together with statuettes, gems and coins which convey only an incomplete and inaccurate idea of what they must have looked like. In recompense, there survive important remains of the sculpture decorating the great temple of Athena on the Acropolis, the Parthenon. Built between 447 and 432 B.C. at the behest of Pericles, the political leader of the Athenian city state, with the constant collaboration of Phidias, its decorative scheme combining statues in the round and reliefs was conceived and to a large extent carried out under his supervision. It provides an accurate idea of the immense scope of his genius despite the uneven passages resulting from the lesser talents of the different artists working under his direction. The frieze of bas-reliefs which ran right round the building above the sides and the doors on the inside provides the best opportunity for a definition of the classical style as developed by Phidias and transmitted to the rest of Greece. A nobility of form and inspiration, a harmony of composition, a subtle and varied sense of movement in the representation of groups and individuals, a living perfection in the portrayal of nudes and a plastic richness in the draped figures—all these are the essence of a style in which freedom of movement never detracts from dignity. Attic sculpture was profoundly influenced by the Parthenon, as witness the famous relief found at Eleusis (Plate 21) on which the three figures of gods could well have been taken straight from the frieze of the Parthenon so much do they share the spirit that informs it.

An entire category of sculptures existed during this period which, because of their function, were highly susceptible to the influence of Phidias: these were the funerary stelae which were erected over graves. Greek beliefs about the survival of the soul after death were far from consoling since they promised only a wretched existence in Hades among the other shades accompanied by an eternal nostalgia for the pleasures of life on earth. The feeling that death was a final and irrevocable separation was at the forefront of the Greek mind however ready they may have seemed to be to resign themselves to the laws governing human existence. The art of Phidias provided them with a language which enabled them to visualise this awareness with intense feeling. The funerary stelae usually show the dead man in an attitude of serene meditation accompanied by a servant or surrounded by relatives but with no special features to distinguish him from them. The veneration due to the dead who are no longer present and for that very reason share to some degree in the awe-inspiring powers of the life beyond the grave is mingled in these sculptures with a subdued sadness. The reserve and modesty with which this sorrow is expressed endow them with a silent eloquence which is still profoundly moving.

After the period dominated by Phidias (c. 450-400 B.C.), which was also strikingly characterised by its artistic unity, Greek art became at once more complex and more varied. The dominance of Athens which had enabled Phidias to influence all Greece, gave way to endless divisions between the different city states, with the advantage passing from one to another until the Macedonian dynasty emerged under Philip and Alexander the Great. This period of unrest was a time of great intellectual ferment and scientific research, producing Aristotle and Plato to name only two of its greatest thinkers. Older systems of thought were called in question and fresh ones created. The art of the period expresses in its variety the same willingness to examine all phenomena anew, as well as the feverish nature of the search.

Already, in the closing years of the fifth century B.C., some sculpture reveals a desire to escape from the serenity of the classical period into the merely pleasing and pretty. An example of this mood can be seen in the graceful gestures of the *Victories* decorating the balustrade which surrounds the small temple known as the temple of Athena Nike near the entrance to the Acropolis (Plate 23). This search for gracefulness as an embellishment of a life that was far from being free of anxiety led to an interest in the theme of childhood which had never greatly attracted the sculptors of preceding periods. There are a few fine examples in the images of small girls found at Brauron in Attica in a sanctuary dedicated to Artemis, which admirably convey the charm of early youth. Early adolescence also interested an artist like Praxiteles who produced many variations on this one theme. The bronze recovered from the sea near Marathon (Plate 24) belongs to the same group of sculptures and clearly shows the influence of this great Athenian sculptor. It portrays Hermes in the posture evoked in a well-known Homeric Hymn. He holds in his left hand a tortoise shell (this has not survived) and delighted by this find which will provide him with a sounding board for his lyre he gaily snaps the fingers of his right hand in a spontaneous expression of joy. The intensely human character of this gesture is as revealing of the new objects of the artists' curiosity as the elegance and grace of the youthful god.

This bronze *Hermes* sharply contrasts with another bronze, also found in the sea near the small island of Anticytherea. It dates from roughly the same period, and portrays a powerful athlete, but his proportions are designed to produce an ultimate impression of elegance (Plate 25). This is the statue discussed earlier which represents Hercules in the Garden of the Hesperides plucking the apple of immortality. It gives a glimpse into the world of the supernatural but, at this later stage of Greek religion, a supernatural in which there is a message of consolation in that Hercules is a type of the righteous man. The sculptor is clearly embodying the hopes and aspirations of his fellow men. This statue is as rich in symbolic meaning as it is in aesthetic value. It is undeniably the work of a great artist and could well be attributed to Skopas, a complex genius who flourished in the middle of the fourth century B.C. Together with Praxiteles and Lysippos he forms a brilliant trio which was the object of constant admiration in the ancient world. Unfortunately, we know nothing of their work except at second hand through inferior copies produced during the Roman period, which all too often can only tentatively be identified. Beyond doubt, the richness of plastic art during the fourth century derives from the contribution of these outstanding talents. After this period, and in contrast to preceding periods, a genuine period style is no longer discernible and this prevents the accurate dating of unknown works. Instead there were produced works by the combined efforts of several master sculptors or works in different styles produced at exactly the same time and these provided models that were copied by lesser artists according to their own inclinations or those of their clients. For this reason the tracing of stylistic influences and their inter-relationships becomes increasingly complex: the works of previous periods were copied in a spirit of more or less deliberate pastiche and archaic styles coexisted with genuine experimental work.

This complexity inevitably renders the task of the historian of art even more difficult, but what can be made clear, thanks to the wide variety of the works which have survived, is the amazing diversity of fourth-century sculpture. The numerous funerary stelae lost none of the quietly moving eloquence that characterised those produced by earlier periods. The statues of gods, and particularly goddesses, develop further in the direction of youthful grace as witness the bronze *Athena*, found recently in Piraeus, whose finely-drawn features are very different from the majestic creations of Phidias. This statue, like many others produced at the same time, reveals how the gap between the divine and the human has been narrowed and this is further borne out by a comparison between the *Athena* and the statue of the young woman with her hair arranged in the melon-shaped hair-style which was found at the same time. The gods draw closer to men during this period: is the well-known marble head from Tegea that of a goddess or a mortal woman? It is hard to say and this very ambiguity is in itself revealing. On the other hand, a statue of a boxer (Plate 27) visibly marked by the blows he has received in fights reveals the progress towards a realism that is very far from the earlier traditions, preoccupied as they were with the idealisation of the human form.

The death of Alexander the Great in 323 B.C. is usually taken as a convenient starting point of the following period—usually known as the Hellenistic period—which lasted until the beginning of the Roman Empire with the battle of Actium in 31 B.C. After this period, Greek art, far from disappearing, continued to develop with an undimmed brilliance but within the political and social framework of Roman imperialism. The change of historical perspective this implies enables us to place a term to Greek art in the fullest sense at the end of the first century B.C. During the three centuries that passed between the reign of Alexander and that of Augustus the complexity of different influences and of experimentation is even more marked than it was during the fourth century B.C. The study of this period is far from complete because accurately-dated works are rare and the lines of development are of a daunting complexity. Many works, while revealing fine workmanship, continue the academic traditions of the past. Others show originality but at the cost of taste and proportion, revealing a tendency towards turgid inflation and bombastic flamboyance that is especially apparent in certain statues of gods such as the *Poseidon* of Milo (Plate 29) whose theatrical posture contrasts unfavourably with the regal authority of the *Poseidon* of Histiaea. Something akin to the baroque emerged during this period, a style that strained after effect for its own sake, a style moreover that exerted considerable influence upon the art of the Roman period and through that upon the European Renaissance. Other artists devoted their talent to anecdotal works, depicting the trivia of day-to-day life, the picturesque qualities of life in the streets. This mood produced strange and occasionally appealing works such as the small bronze jockey of the second century B.C. (Plate 30). The anecdotal, ignored during the classical period, became predominant.

Finally, special mention should be made of the portrait which, rare in the fifth century, became more frequent in the fourth, when much more interest was taken in the individual for his own sake. Portrait sculpture became more popular still during the Hellenistic period when men were emerging from the narrow confines of the city state and affirming their claim to an existence independent of the group. The high quality of these late portraits (Plates 31 and 32) gives the lie to the assertion that this was a period of artistic decadence.

This brief historical survey gives a general idea only of the extraordinary richness of Greek art. It will have served its purpose if it whets the reader's appetite for learning more. The sculpture reproduced in the illustrations has preserved the inner essence of a people with whom we are able to feel a sense of genuine kinship because of the skill of the artists among them. It is up to us to listen to what they have to tell us from beyond the gulf of the centuries so miraculously spanned by the art they created.

ILLUSTRATIONS

4

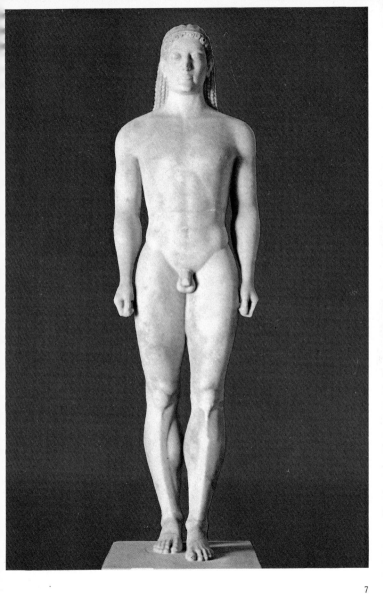

14

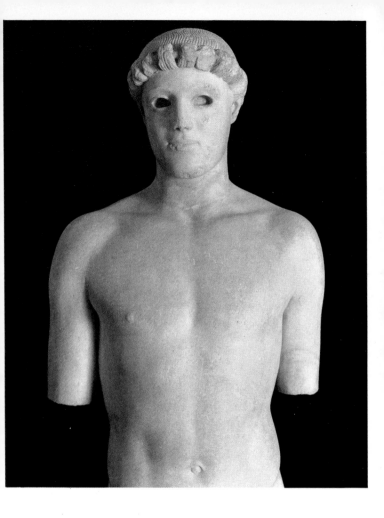

17

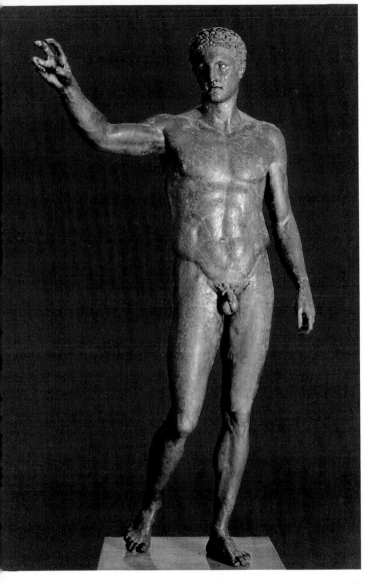

CONTENTS

———

* *Translated from the French*

CONTENTS

The colour photographs of this volume were specially taken by Mario Carrieri.

BIBLIOGRAPHY

General Works

CHAMOUX, François, *Art grec*, Milan-Paris-Lausanne, 1966.

GINOUVÈS, René, *L'Art grec*, Paris, Presses Universitaires de France, 1964.

HAFNER, German, *Geschichte der griechischen Kunst*, Zurich, Atlantis Verlag. 1961.

POULSEN, Vagn, *Griechische Kunst*, Königstein-in-Taunus, Langewiesche, 1962.

RICHTER, Gisela M. A., *A Handbook of Greek Art*, London, Phaidon Press, 1959.

Greek Sculpture

ADAM, S., *The Technique of Greek Sculpture in the Archaic and Classical Periods*, London, Thames & Hudson, 1966.

BIEBER, Margarete, *The Sculpture of the Hellenistic Age*, New York, Columbia University Press, 1955.

BLÜMEL, K., *Griechische Bildhauer an der Arbeit*, third edition, Berlin, W. de Gruyter, 1945.

CARPENTER, Rhys, *Greek Sculpture*, Chicago, The University of Chicago Press, 1960.

CHARBONNEAUX, Jean, *La Sculpture grecque archaïque*, Paris, 1945.

CHARBONNEAUX, Jean, *la Sculpture grecque classique*, 2 vols., Paris, 1943-1946.

CHARBONNEAUX, Jean, *Les Bronzes grecs*, Paris, Presses Universitaires de France, 1958.

HANFMANN, G.M.A., *Classical Sculpture*, New York, 1967.

LIPPOLD, G., *Die griechische Plastik*, Munich, 1950.

PICARD, Charles, *Manuel d'archéologie grecque. La Sculpture*, 7 vols., Paris, Editions A. et J. Picard, 1935-1963.

RICHTER, Gisela M. A., *The Sculpture and Sculptors of the Greeks*, third edition, New Haven, Yale University Press, 1950.

RICHTER, Gisela M. A., *The Portraits of the Greeks*, 3 vols., London, Phaidon Press, 1965.

SCHUCHHARDT, Walter-Herwig, *Die Epochen der griechischen Plastik*, Baden-Baden, Grimm, 1959.

Printed in Italy